The
DOUBLE
PIPES
of PAN

ARLENE STONE

The DOUBLE PIPES PIPES of PAN

North Atlantic Books
Berkeley, California

Publisher's Address:

North Atlantic Books
2320 Blake Street
Berkeley, California 94704

Cover Design: Paula Morrison
Cover Photograph: Jerry Stoll

The author gratefully acknowledges *Contact II, Thirteenth Moon, Poetry Now,*
and *Pudding,* in which some of the poems from this collection were first
published.

The Double Pipes of Pan is sponsored by the Society for the Study of Native
Arts and Sciences, a nonprofit educational corporation whose goals are to
develop an ecological and crosscultural perspective linking various scientific,
social, and artistic fields; to nurture a holistic view of arts, sciences, humani-
ties, and healing; and to publish and distribute literature on the relationship
of mind, body, and nature.

This project was partially supported by a grant from the National Endowment
for the Arts, Washington, D.C.

Library of Congress Cataloging in Publication Data

Stone, Arlene.
    The double pipes of Pan.

    I. Title.
PS3569.T6294D6 1983   811'.54   83-13435
ISBN 0-938190-18-0 (pbk.)

CONTENTS

I

II

III

I

The Double Pipes of Pan

At your table   the door to a temple
hearing your sound tapes
the maddened goats who were men
hearing mere girls blow through
the Sapphic ear of conch shells

& the flutes
the flutes ecstatic hooves
tattooing my skin
smoke escalating the Andes
crumbling stone tablets
Macchu Picchu
last fortress for the besieged

You talking repression
the way women wait at the threshold
afraid to enter the snail hut at Uxmal
that womb whose winding stair is passion

At your table   studying order
Perpendicular line-ups
        the high-towered sombreros
        the tiny gold-lipped Bible
        the woven birds whose legs were needles
        intermittent with threads
        the dry leather couch   its absence of semen
Objects composed as carefully
as your scores

How the vegetables smiled
from the saffron you poured on their faces
the plates sun-soaked at twilight
as though hope
were the state of our world

Once
upstairs in the bowel of this
upside-down universe
hearing men pray on brain level
on my behalf   to their god
I watched angels who were not my children
cavort on cloud-painted eaves

Leaving your threshold
high on mushroom and sesame chutney
and conversation coca
descending your saffron mountain
to the king in synthetic tiger pelt
who dozed in my bed
Suckling his pipes as he entered
my snail house   that cauldron
Eating my flavor off his fingers
Watching black mustard seed dance
as it seduced the white in the rice

Fearing you   woman
who were I myself
longing to climb you with gay abandon
Woman
you were Peru

Iphigenia

I handed her over
the sun in my eyes
I couldn't see them go
through the doorway omphalos
& back along the sea path
long & curled as a birth cord

I know she walked out to greet him
as I instructed
she lithe as a flower underwater
succulents braided in her hair
swayed when his tentacle
touched her
inked by that squid
who came to the women's house
to demand her
to propitiate the fathers

I followed them to the platform
            Was it forbidden?
divesting myself of my skin
petal
        by petal
tearing my hair for grass
I climbed the stone stairs
back through a thousand decades
I wove   in my female cycle
a carpet of ruby tears
the fields green as a cemetery
the hill high as a birth pain
the day black as a crow's throat
when it happened

It was not I who made the cut
nor pulled the heart from its nest
a virgin dove

I know it followed me back
where I gave myself to the man
in the moon again
& again
Her heart   that was Darkness
peered at me from his forehead
wrapped in gauze moonlight
a jewel on a crown

He is not to be blamed
I dragged my leg irons to his bed
to enter his stomach
fat & full
I might have wished for a sword

It will follow me all my days
the high noon black in blood
crushing the sun's head between its legs
& dazzling as the orb's last rays
the blade
poised between two starry spheres
Then the plunge
when the sun went into the house
that was Midnight

Yes
Bacchus bit the grape
& put out all the stars

Heart
say I was not there
his hand digging into my womb
his knife in the witch's coven

Husband?

Daughter
Daughter

Independence Day Overture

Daddy Death
my maestro

In this dream you took
the hands from the face of
the clock that was moon
took my key ring
that womb
leaving me locked
in a *do-re-mi* room

Tut Arthur cum Fiedler come
Does the dream never close
In this grave the wound turns

Dum dum
Dum dum

Down river a cannon
Boom
Boom

to your 1912 overture

The smoke clears away
I am picking the shell
from my teeth/cunt/tongue

I have eaten the baby
Too late   Hubby Dumb

Last Tango

Who planned this diabolic funeral
for still virile soul
this catered wedding with
the former husband

My mother waits to monogram
two sofas with his name
The name tags wait
like all the curses hemmed
upon our children's clothing
to forward them to summer

& I'm to stitch these skin grafts
on the cushions
to get our lover off
to Satan's boot camp

Too late to cancel now
He'll show up with his second wife
& Mother & I shall dance
the anniversary waltz for the bereft
& eat fastidiously
the canapés of seasoned flesh

Mother & I shall dance
like two black candles
sleek and naked
before the hee-haw relatives
claws digging in
upon each other's back to gain
a foothold

Perhaps
I should let that ailing lady rest
& pirouette a broom
around the room

This is the second time
we booked the hall
The lights refuse to speak
above a whisper
The shades are lowered to half-mast
I dare not lift them
for fear some men outside
have carried off the sky
& set it up to be
our cemetery tent

We woke at dawn
& dressed as woodenly as dolls
For years we have sat here
& waited for the mourners' limousine
while in the mouldy hall
Memory plays
and everlastingly replays
Hate's *pizzicato*
& the raucous roaches tango

Cormorants

Putting on feather gloves
for the first time in ten years

she dialed his number
His voice throbbed like a heart

with angina
She would have massaged that muscle

She thought she had dialed love
but his words blew poison darts

through the wires
while hers whirled confusedly

as tin cans thrown up
only to be shot down

Then a wing swept away the receiver
Words suctioned her into space

Clawing the sky
down she followed him

onto the brine foul with droppings
to pounce on their prey

& as she bit the neck
swift as a jellyfish sting

thought how
she had managed to navigate

through the static
enlisting his help

for the first time in a decade
her tongue their

daughter's tombstone
his mouth a womb of blood

Helpless

Knee-deep in soiled wash
you are drowning
the dishes unscraped
& the dust thick enough to talk to
Outdoors the hills cave in
Indoors is a pressure cooker
the mirrors cracked
with the creases in old skin

You are not old
a woman in the daisy knot of
samplered life
the room so cold it could
be full of falling snow
your name written clearly
in English or Hebrew
a prophecy some moving finger left
on a frosted New England window

This room could be ice
& you the sculpture of a dying swan
or I five hundred miles away
or five million
for all the difference it makes

yet say I were here
in this room
we know I would not lift
a pricked finger to help you
as you wound about your neck
your father's sleeve
the father I chose for you

I lick the thread
I steady the needle
I put up water to boil
so not to hear you gurgle

Why did I bring you
O hook
into the eye of my world

Storm at Half Moon Bay

Never have you looked so lovely
as you do in grief
features wooden yet noble
a figurehead sawed off a prow
half a dozen years after launching

Wild the celadon green of the eye
Grey your pallor as the sky
that appears to hold
every tear back
an optical trick of light

and distance
the sand two days before Christmas
dark as burnt pumpkin
rimmed by dead gulls or walnuts
where small shore birds huddle

grouped for holiday pie
Gales pellet the restaurant window
Cold penetrates the panes
a noxious gas
the heart a boat pounded in harbor

Only four in the afternoon
yet the birds close their eyes
tiny house lights blinking out
all along the shore
Quelled the most activist beak

except for the tide
raising the water's windswept hair
No trace left from what sky wings
were fleshed by clouds
storm riding the California coast

an impenitent father ghost
Candles quiver in cut-glass hands
the waitress nondescript as a shell
the rock-fish tasteless
as supper prepared by a taxidermist

My pearl
again we are bound for
the River of Woe
fish skeletons feasting
on human bone

Sotto Voce

The patient tells it the way it was
The family refuses to listen
to bend down to the well level

Must she scream above their complaints
that she won't talk to them
who mutters all the time
an infant of twenty-nine
her own child sold to its father
for less than silver

She whispers
They talk
How she gave the child to them
& wants it back
her nervous hands kneading
the dress in her lap
her torso rocking
birth's water bed
their voices a ward
of unfed babies

Can you hear her
drawing upon the bucket
whose vocal cord snapped
tugging
& tugging
at the umbilical strands
in her lap

Weird Sister

Refusing the drug
the patient tries reason
reminds them of her right
to refuse food/pills/needles
reminds them of her right
not to be manhandled
or abused
the woman small
the two men chosen for
their size
as they close in
reminds them of
her right
her right
her right
jumps from the bed
seizes a corner
prays
recites spells
hisses
as they advance
casts herself into
the last ditch
the magic they call
crazy

Two South

It begins with a chain of steps
a locked steel door at the top
This is not the end
Beyond are the palsied hands
the swollen faces of mostly women
in county nightgowns
shufflling hunchbacks
with boils on their feet
one a large brown otter
hair set in clothespins
another an old white crow who sings
hello hello hello
one spilled on a bed
puddled soda or urine
the night stand mouldy
& a wardrobe
with no place to hang

Macho

Coward you call me
as you come at me

Am I to slay you
who say you want children

Are you not too a woman
who bleeds as the moon

spins like a tarnished penny
into a black velvet purse

Waking tonight
my lover cold

& smooth as marble
the city lights blinking off

blinking on
like the foregone race they are

I am buried alive
your curses thick as stars

Links

It was my mother then
who sent the letters pitched

to the wastebasket
my mother who called twice a day

to a padlocked phone
my mother whose jaw was frozen

who bribed pain with a heating pad
my mother who heard the snake lady

hiss in solitary
while the other slept on

a pink elephant drugged
with candy pills

The chant goes up
The golden choker closes

I join the electric circle
taking hold of my mother's hand

A Dress for my Daughter's Eyes

I have bought my daughter a cumquat sheath
the fabric is juiced with berry
darkened by bleeding greens
& damariscotta plum
& bluebird indigo
The sun is in its ruffle stilled
& lies upon its hammock
Its straps are fine as spider lines
that spin-off from my daughter's eyes

The first time I looked into
the miraculous shrine of daughter eyes
through Czarist butterfly wings
into the whirling citrine fizz
into the Siberian mousse
into the jade for a thousand Taoist faces
into those green thumbs
into glass palace green-houses

my daughter's eyes bade me rise from the bed
where I trucked my ikons
the dead
the dead

Today is a day for miracles
for I had bequeathed my daughter
sorrow and melancholia
Their fallout covered my pillow
I had seen them in hallways tied to tubes
I who had tasted the blood
of my living mother
& lived

Today I saw a woman who wept
from plastic eye-cups
a woman whose bones were sieves
whose sinews as lead
& my friend requested
champagne & *hors d' oeuvres* be brought

Today   in a rubber tub
where last month palm had withered
a seed nine months gestated put out leaves
& a striped petunia flourished
Today I spoke to my daughter
three thousand miles away
& my daughter said
I am happy

Today I bought her a firefly sheath
to wear over the moonlight's
multiple slips
May no moths move in to deface us

Batik

Fluid as hot paraffin we stand
brushing the silk length
with wax warm as a hand
the cloth a sea we cause to ripple
Tacked to saw-horses it dips
on waves gentle as evening

A robe for a priestess
or Danäe waking
or Martha Graham in one of
her stately geisha dances
Shadows lend solidity to forms
that do not heal themselves
Light gives a third dimension
the night takes back

To define where vibration ends
& void begins
To finish the form while staying
within the lines
our medium faulty on fingers
that try for perfect coverage
Foxglove violet dogwood & gentian
leaves under our brushes
darken in descent

The door opens to moth flurry
the wax unstable at melting point
the dye with a will of her own
filling in a death mask
to be consumed by acid

This room is a garden of wax
my dears
& we opaque with exhaustion
as candles without fire
all our years of design
a surface merely
our patient & painstaking work
washed away like tears

Caesarian

A red-headed flower is sitting there
Near her a young man hovers
He wants to marry her
though she is years older
Mother says she approves
of the match

Have they told him
she had two children by marriage
He will see the knife lines
on her stomach
white as sweet butter

Wait
something went wrong with
the operation
The patient is losing color

Mother
Close up your womb
Clamp back the turf
Our rose of Sharon
two years is dead
Rebirth   that dream
does not work

Sisters

Was there ever a time when
friendship between us was possible

Even now you are ill I feel I am winning
a competition begun with your birth

Imagining your difficult breath
smoke from the throat of a cigarette

I feel unable to breathe & when I look
for the sky I see clouds painted in

on a ceiling
To be trapped like ozone in the atmosphere

by the inability to act
or when we move   to get our faces slapped

by cold air currents
To eat to sleep

To extend through sleep that
consummation called grief

All this at a time when sisters
have never done more to help one another

At the next table a sister
holds another's thighs

& in the back room   sisters
move to harmonies

their hands upon another's back
are swaying leaves

They kiss each other on the mouth
as some kiss men

& if they leave   they leave together
as houses who go side by side

on an insistent tide
But you & I   within our separate walls

are last to sleep
We wake within our crumbling bodies

homeless   godless as ghosts
in this ungodly hour

Swan Song

The window is closed
as the mother watches the daughter

waltz in the garden
with the hose that is swan

the mother tapping her toes
pumping the heart's barrel organ

Ballads
of blood and women

Swan lifting his head
from breast meadows

the swan a copperhead
the mother's breath a snare drum

Snake
mistaking the beat

of fear for fury
lets out a long red hiss

The daughter is closed like a book
The mother opens the sky

II

Never Never Land

Are you the prince
I lived with yesterday
who today meets me
with cross-bow drawn
behind a mile-high moat?

You say there is no moat
and raise your draw-bridge
Oh   there is no draw-bridge?
And the castle?
There was no castle?

No prince or princess?
No turrets raised
in twin defense
when nighthood was
in never flower?

Second Period: Castle

He will come on a cotton cloud
He will come on the back of a sheep
to a quacking of pottery ducks

He will wear a butterscotch beret
He will play Olde English sword dances
on an Appalachian dulcimer

She will wait like a crumbling crumpet
or a feather parrot perched
on a quilted satin star

She will yawn till the Ice Age
flows again and freezes over
into an earth that is swan

> *Why are you waiting*
> *my feather frump*
> *Why are you waiting*
> *my sugar lump*

The new Grimm says
Pegasus comes in a Concorde jet
to carry her off to a gingerbread fret

a castle charged on Mastercharge
where they have child analogues
through the Whole Earth Catalog

Towers

You in your chainmail
I in my hair-shirt named Longing
imprisoned in a tower
built well before the Middle Age
its stairs concealed ingeniously

From this height I survey
the perilous moats that mark Passion Land
My tower is not impregnable
Its walls are skin
skin the key to its drawbridge

I am talking as if
there were not the hundred
winding steps from the plain
where on your horse named Coffee
you survey the woman towers
that beckon long-gloved fingers
on midnight's jewelled wrist

each unique
in buttresses or battlements
or half-barrel vaults
or with tiny vaulted chapels
or hidden windows
or arrow slits

You'll follow any hem
that clarions the dust
swearing fealty to all
a dog that must stop at each bush
for a whiff of its own rank perfume

Let's stop this medieval conceit

You call to me from across the pool
Your song is not the nightingale's
I am not in haircloth but cotton
The plain is an apartment complex

but the night is lovely
dark & deep
The rivals sleep like sacristies
You are Love in his bullet-proof robe

Nightland

Sitting at night on the bridge
that demarcates friend from lover
dangling our feet

giving them time to decide
whether to go back the way they came
or advance into the tenuous land

where touch is reconciled with feeling
like light with dark
at the horizon

Stepping down uneasily
into the leafy grotto
the trees a green memorized

& blotted out
their trunks dark hairs
magnified a million times

the sky too remote to consider
the brook noise remote
as the suck of a sleeping child

You say you want an affair
You say you are married
Black slashes outline you

You said there were no
wild animals here
my crouching bear

Blonde Branches in Formal Meter

Sunset golding the leaves on the olive
silvering your bushy crown
Kenny Rogers singing   *Ruby*
please   don't take your love to town

You get up to change the record   turn
sun plucking chords along your back
shoulder arch tapering roundly to hip
light recording you on 8 track

No way   Ruby   to slow down the sunset
No way to turn back the war on a watch
Fire glows on the house in the valley
your eye accidentally lighting my match

Saturday Morning

Lying naked on my belly on your terrace
eating Velveeta cheese on crackers
listening to The Eagles
letting the sun sneak through my legs
to lick the place you licked
with your long cat tongue
for breakfast

Studying your red neck
the strawberry rash at the crease
behind your knee
your muscled legs
hair homely as seaweed
the handsome Jimmie Dean head
the thick thatch
the smouldering dimple in your chin
the soft flop of your sex
its raspberry sugarcone ring

It's nearly time to go

Closing my eyes
holding on to your ankle or wrist

Welcome to The Hotel California

*You can check out but you
can never leave*

Dinner Party

We commingle
spoons & forks
bumping

& jangling
you stroking that
other woman's handle

while showing me
only your
tines

Minnie in the Meat Maze

Sluggish in your recliner
of imitation rawhide
torpid as a boulder
or an earth-moving equipment
turning your back on the mind
& the wind bells of exercise
you snore clogged dust & lava bubbles
Mount St. Helen's ready to erupt
Your rhythmic theme is
   work
   sleep
   eat
monotonous as TV

Good minotaur
feasting on your own surplus
like an old rubber tire
you wallow in dream mud
a cannibal in Fat Swamp

Caught in the sludge I sigh
Down with the Vegetable Empire

Meat

I a slender asparagus stalk
lithe as a birch rod
you a fat side of beef

I could slice right through you
with my eager beaver lettuce teeth
I could grind you in my burger pit

but
being a vegetarian
pacific as a pond
       Monet lilies loll in my mouth
       eggplant purple
       celery & spinach green
       the mayonnaise whites
       shimmer like birds-of-paradise

You eat little birds
You know you do
You bake them in Mother Goose pie
or roast them whole as hearts o my
you who are shaped like rib steak
who weigh on me dark & dense
as an African rhino

I yield to your tongue
Red as a stripe in the flag I come
sizzling with fireworks fat
my artichoke soul gazing down
on a flank of spoiled beef
the I who was war
& am meat

Mulatto

Butter & sugar they call it
where I come from in Massachusetts
corn with a different father from mother
a half-breed next to its midwestern cousins
whose faces are blah as white suburbs

Around Rock Island Illinois
where you swam the Mississippi mud
to sneak wet & hide
from your mother's belt
that lynch rope
A thousand miles of corn
Sun spikes the field's barbed helmet
motorbike revved to go
where booze & sex are the only speeds
& you called the woman of color
you loved up *nigger*
& still wonder why she robbed you blind

Color in Dick
Color in Jane
who looked & felt black
when she married each night
a red-neck bull she hoped
to breed into a unicorn
with a single horn
that the body & mind
the act & the word
the life & the art
might be one

Barter

Over the olive tree's shoulder
three apartment flights down

in the dark bushy pubes
two men argue over a woman

she taciturn
as the evergreen

Come with me
I'm your friend   companion

his buddy's beerbelly white
as a Scorpio moon

in the twisted hair
of a cornfield

She's not yours   She's mine
I'll sell her to you

for a hundred dollars
the olive tree flinching

as the wind's rifle
fires a volley

Redneck

The flush seeps in from the jowl
flooding your face with napalm
The fire behind you has swamped
a delta in Asia

& you
the man from my village
I called *brother*
                    uncle
                            lover
                                    friend
you who condone the murder
of a Martin Luther King

The hands that touch my intimate parts
would pull the trigger
or tighten the rope
would scream obscenities with the mob
as I went up in a tree
or down in a ditch
men with your face boning me
front to rear

A quartered fowl
I saw this woman recently
on a Hustler magazine cover

But it isn't you   you said

& how would you know me
in the dark in a hollow city
Pinned under you I'd see only the eye
a bloodshot flag
the neck a nuclear test-tube

Heavyweights

We have been training for eons
from the time the Earth was a crystal egg
before birds conceived of metal
up through the dinosaurs & dire wolves
through Cleopatra & Antony
through black as Iago ages
through Eldridge Cleaver flooring his wife

This is a game for pros
It goes beyond the limits
up through the tenth round
It doesn't end with lost milk teeth
or skinned knees or cracked ribs
or stars gouged out like eyes
from an Oedipal sky

Sure
we've kayoed the famous
Our faces show the erosion
They resemble cauliflower from some
primeval garden   white lava fistlets
powdered with ash

Tonight our sparring is over
The Garden is packed   the bets all in
The ticket prices set by scalpers
have passed the nuclear threshold

When the bell rings
come out from your corner
I'm the rival you've always been out
to take   the bitch with suckling pups
here in the Arena   under the Goddess eye
pitiless as the light over an operating table

Tall & fiery as the True Cross you circle
your arms & legs blazing brands
your head black as a burnt-out match
your flesh as white as a sheet
your neck as red as my monthly blood
your hands the rope about the nigger's throat

Harley

"It's only Low Rider, you and the open road"
(From a Harley Davidson ad)

Masturbating its own length
the open road swells & extends

Safe in your matched leathers
the scarred hide fuming
buckhorn handlebars aimed
lone as a sailor at sea
lashed to the mast between your legs
a stump of custom iron

Junk food stops
Hot & cold blondes
Parades of T-shirts opening
easy as picked locks
Dynamite days pulse-pounding as Dolly Parton
The mountains fat pink grapefruits
& the ocean's blue clitoris
riding the pink sugar dunes

Toward evening   rain
as the wasted sun
finds a cheap motel to party in

Night's chilled beer cans foaming over
Nights that fizz with stars
Night   the long-stemmed babe
in a short mildewed towel
Night   the ice machine that vomits
diamonds   hearts & bad-ass doobies

You party with Night
the black-mustachioed Paladin
Nine wins in a row
"Nine spoke wheels spinning you forward"
You lose your old lady at cards
You lose your partner to some bad speed

Back of the eight-ball   Harley
luck grabbing your balls
every motel a dump
a toothless mother in every driveway
her bones poke through her housedress
like No Vacancy signs

& the rats
the rats as white as sand
rats in your tool kit
rats in your gear
rats that chew through your beer cans
faster than a church key

the miles bumpy now
grip greasy with pork rinds
& behind each jog
the pigs in their cages
tuning in to radar
Behind each bend the dog packs
ropes to lassoo your kidneys
or bite your wheels

Beside you the skeleton rides
yelling *Seig Heil*
The sun leaks like Three Mile Island
Wolf jowls rainburst the clouds
You twist full throttle

  Sixty
   Seventy
    Eighty
     Ninety
the sky a gyreing black mustache
     One hundred
     One ten

the roadsides closing in a zippering fly
the bike in its teeth
throbbing

Sky Woman Loses Control

The night you stood me up
& I lost my birth control
I hit the trail to find you
my clit erect as a Cheyenne war-bonnet

In a Gary Cooper movie I saw you
making whoopee with a squaw
whose sex was deep as a disappeared ocean
my horse named Wrath so swift
I dropped the magic ring I carried
      the hoop for my womb
       the basket for seed
        the medicine bag
        with miracle jellies
      to ward off making little clouds

I should have stayed in the wigwam
& prayed to The Evening Star
that by the light of his sister
The Morning
you would appear on your cloud horse
with your peace-pipe for me to smoke

Bad

That time we did it in the closet
dark as a drawer

the workmen thought we were out in the yard
watching the landlady

tie a daisy to a stake
like an impotent husband

the closet dark as a book read under the covers
Make believe there's a ship

In a lifeboat on deck two kids hide
from Daddy & Mommy

who waltz to sound by a rock & roll ocean
their patter far off as rain to a cave

Bat wings beat at hearts of darkness
spasms clenched between their legs

those jaws pried open at night
Make believe you are in a crib

next to the night-stand where
the bad books are kept

closing your eyes to the mattress
where witches whisper through horsehair

the rank air webbed with spells
Years later

hot as a haystack on fire
riding your cockhorse to Orgasm Gorse

the bats are all teeth
the closet a haunted house

The Olives

The olives outside your window
needled by rain
& sun-glinted as grass

in Paradise
The branches upon the olives
that undulate suavely

as I on this waterbed
you left hours ago
reluctant to wake while

cradled by motion
The olives' rhythm last night
when we made love

& you were very satisfied
& I was not so quite
the clouds as clumsy then

as hunches by a primitive painter
blunt white upon a swarthy
canvas sky

one star as clear
as the many displayed now
on shimmering trays

gems that massed as we slept
fallen angels who daubed
the trees with their

profane glass beads
the ripe fruit never
to be picked or cured

while far below
between the arboral stalks
mesmeric in dance

as bamboo groves
lovers walk the paths
that gleam with fecund leaves

walk matter-of-fact as birds
who toe & squash
the olives fat & black

as water bugs
& roll the pits upon their
insteps like dead souls

Topping Lake Tahoe

Back to the darkened dance floor
Back to the disco beat
Back to gyrating before God's disc jockey

we who cruised the whiskey browns of Gold Country
where John Wayne never lost a wheel
& those in the Donner wagon train
(mired gulls on the ice-veined passes)
mistook each other for food

Returned on the wind's roulette wheel
to throw the dice
in the same combinations we'd left
Back to deal stale decks
the cards marked with old cave symbols
Back to the bed   that casino

come raining silver dollars
our slot machines wild
we are fucking the odds
gamblers out for cold cash
your ace in my hole
& the Dealer is hot

That Creepy Peeping Tom in our Bed

The one who lives in the closet & waits
to be let out   That Dr. Hyde

dependent on the good nature of Jekyll
That full-sized doll we gave light to

though I don't remember birthing him
He was smuggled in here by you   my friend

Who knows how long he lay there
playing with himself

before you introduced the hustler
that Prince from Hollywood

a rubber duckie
who's larger in girth

than his flesh & blood daddy
& with a buzz a bee would envy

& a sting   that incites
my mountainsprings to run uphill

into the cup of your hand   until
we pull him off & cast him aside

to do what men & women do
once they've put back childhood

Poison Oak Beach

For months in our birthday clothes
we lay on the beach
among the gasping coals
red rocks called love or passion
neglecting sun screen cream
exposed to gamma rays
& blistering creep of plants
along the steep path down
to doze under the solar lamp
& wake as basket cases

I moved into your apartment
You moved into my house
We spent a lot of time in bed
Arguments mounted
acrobats standing each
on shoulders below
resentments settling in
like sand between the toes

The worst is over
the phase they call bright pink
the pain & painful antidotes to pain
analyses   those vinegar baths
apologies   those ointment rubs
fucking   the analgesic we over-dosed on

Outside the house window
the bay is motionless
no   not quite
From the direction of the bridge
a small skiff prods the water
fly nudging a sleeping body

Today   straight as a broom
you returned to work minus your limp
& I have spent the morning
sweeping the floor of our lost skin

A Convention of Clowns

We are pitched into a party
The Big Top is spinning
The cocktails have motion sickness
The tent walls are soft as cheese

You have combed the floss over your bald spot
I have rouged fever globes on my cheeks
& underlined my eyebrows with awed white

You take one ring
I take another   competing for laughs
We juggle our cracker bones
& laugh as they crumble

Is there nothing we will not do
for laughs
You will hug everyone in sight
I will talk in hot air balloons
You carry a toy sword to prick them

My face is red & pregnant
as the backside of a baboon
In a tent full of food I am chewing
plastic wrappers
I am eating pain   it is popcorn
I am puffed like the Fat Lady

Is there nothing we will not do
for pain
You will devour the glass
I hand you
I will laugh at your splintering palate
I will ride your back   O hippo
to dump you
I will even jump through your cut-glass hoop

Our antics get wilder
You sit between a Lioness' thighs
to lick them
I put my head in her mouth
The Lioness is solid brass
her hairs are copper wires
Above her is a giraffe
He is not a midget like you
but tall as a tree in the forest
& the leaves of his hair
would let sun through
if the sun were not charred canvas

I mount the giraffe
You are far below eating the dust
& the children of dust are screeching
God swings over our heads
a papier mâché parrot
with apricot wings & flat button eyes
God swings from a ring
that She for one
does not have to jump through

A whole season has passed since we
somersaulted into this circus
When we stood on our heads
near the entrance
I loved you
We entered the tent as Siamese twins
Our hips held hands like silly putty

Now the happy freaks are severed
In the place of that divine connection
there is only a sumptuous bruise[1]
that peeks through our body stockings

[1]Aubrey Beardsley

Who would recognize in such hunchbacks
who exit singly
twins who raised tents to the stars
We have pulled the stars down on our heads
like acts come up for review

The circus of flesh has had its day
The Theatre of Uglies has scattered
The lords of disorder[2] have lost their titles
Our contract will not be renewed
There are only the pratfalls to tabulate
Can a clown sue a clown for damages?

[2]Wolfgang M. Zucker

III

A Headless Mannequin
Wearing a Red Shoulder Toga

Where nothing is ever completed
everything grows
Your house
with all its beginnings
A headless mannequin
wearing a red shoulder toga
does not have to be human
yet I have this tendency to finish
to close the door
sometimes to lock it

Where nothing is ever hurried
everything waits
Your house
with all its hesitations
A headless mannequin
wearing a red shoulder toga
does not have to be somewhere
yet I have this tendency to place
to move the model
sometimes to dust it

Where nothing is ever put away
everything acts
Your house
with its thousand sideshows
A headless mannequin
wearing a red shoulder toga
does not have to be verbal
yet I have this tendency to brew
to make tea from word roots
sometimes to gulp it

Where everything tastes of jasmine
a headless mannequin
wearing a red shoulder toga
does not have to marry
yet I have this tendency to give her
for face a straw mushroom
Better to leave your house
where stars collect in dishes
rather than try to carry a roof
sometimes to the sky

Houses

This house   the way it gulps
my labor & yet goes hungry
Dust mites eye me with Asian orphan eyes
Surfaces never look clean
though they've just been vacuumed
or scrubbed
& the skin on the knuckles peels
like a lizard's lives
New chips in old paint
Walls I rape just walking by
Floors that age years in an hour
Plants with death rattles
in the Mohave Desert parlor

A house tired as a mother
who never gets well
despite round-the-clock nursing care

Once I had another house
tripled in care by man & child
That house begat two double in size
three houses in all
these walls distant from the pair
by three times a decade
& thrice a thousand miles

Loan shark houses will follow me
to the last furnished room
like cries in a cat fight
ancestors
larger than life

Landlady's Witch Hunt

Gardener that I am
unable to uproot the bush infiltrating
the concrete front sidewalk
or to hack down the golden bamboo
the landlady says will look dead come Fall
or to tear down the shed
shoulder to shoulder with weed
tipsy as neighborhood drunks
supporting each other
downhill
or to rip out the ivies that cling
to the house's old shoe
& the myth of the mother who had so many
she didn't know what to do
or the snails
old grey recluses clutching
their folded shawls
the younger ones basking in solar houses
in the backyard rock garden

Landlady
shall I too be dumped
in the scavenger box by the curb
or just live on here
disturbed

The Piss Ants Move In

Good cat
you sounded the alarm
Ants were marching off
with the kitchen
piss ants
who took two weeks to
size us up for
what we had
worth the taking

Last night they massed
hundreds for a
crumb-to-crumb network
Your dish   that city
is taken
the ant emperor's
retinue a cat spine
inking a snowy
Tokaido highway

Pragmatists survive
us dreamers

You say now the snails
have the garden

Grief for a Feline

Pregnant   they said
when her appetite went bad
& her uterus puffed
a lopsided bean-bag

Pregnant   they said
when she went yellow
as processed cheese food
& the fluid leaked from her

a thin clay slip that bared
a wire armature
Pregnant   they said
when she staggered

like a newborn foal
& fell forward on
her tiny pointed chin
Pregnant

they all concurred
when the film moved
over her eyes
cloudswift across

a darkening sky
Pregnant   read the autopsy
but we who are women
know better

It was not pregnancy
my friends   but blood
& bile   pus that declined
to amber ooze

like fat on soup
What was there
in those crocodile hands
that advanced

to feel
& were unfeeling
What do they see
the veterinarians

& gynecologists
who label poison
in the female
show of life

The Right to Life

The fern spines broken
in trying to rid the garden
of the wild blackberry

The lilac saved
at the expense of the wild bamboo
with golden floss

The ivy pulled
to clear a path through
to the apricot tree

What to kill
& what to save

The Vietnamese civilian
The American soldier

The fetus at conception
The fetus a few weeks later

Roots

Wild as pubic afros
or The Supremes who boogie
into an all-white suburb

you blackberries
ready to pick as poems
the glory of my backyard

have met the fate of the Attica Five
or Inez Garcia when she resisted
a white supremacist

Friends   I intended to make preserves
to keep your memory alive
on my kitchen library shelves

All your exuberance lost
in one landlady's crusade to find
a lost lilac   that *petit bourgeois*

Hacking off legs with a scimitar
or pulling the bud stars out by the hair
to herd them into boxcars

children lost to mothers
husbands to wives
she is proud to bar the foreigners

from her turf
Those that survive the exodus
will die of malnutrition

In her mind a migration problem is solved
but the roots   friends
the roots

A Cursory Look

A fine place to invest in
seeing it from the street side
roofed with red tile in the Spanish style
its many rooms ideal for condominiums

The insurance company refused to pay
Around back the building was black
as a turkey set afire
in a barbecue
entrails trailing relics of empire
refrigerators
toilets
cushions
lumber
the windows eyes relinquished
from their sockets

while we had been ready to buy
our hand reaching into the mailbox
& missing the card at the bottom
Sorry Arlene
I can't see you again

I keep seeing those walls
like a stage set after some play has closed
I keep thinking of the owner
who never got the pay-off
& of the disease that unglues
the body's cellular structure
or how hard it is to write an ending

Season of Diminishment

Little remains
of what we promised ourselves
we'd become
What panic sounded
its moose call
is quelled by the brook
to a gurgle
the will a rosebush
its head under rags
like an injured Bunker
Hill drummer

November noncommittal
leaves drift
toward conclusion
the twigs more talkative
than crows
As the old caretaker
Winter
rounds the path
conscience closes its windows

Darling
even the truth is culpable

The God Box

Sun is trapped in dumb sky
as Eros in stone
the marble slab cold
below her flat buttock

Warmth the squirrel
is gone from these woods
& I am left
holding the tail

Did the sky give away
its eyes as we did
reaching in to touch
our totems in the God Box

If the sky reached into
a pocket of cloud
as your hand through
my heart's scarlet blouse

could it say
as we did
it felt nothing
Liars

Are we trapped by the sun
chips in the sky's blinded eye
Not I   love   Not I
I'll carve my way out

The Woman in the Window

There is a woman who sits
in a chair by a window
watching a woman sit in a chair

her glance a brick
through her window   her mind
the laser cutting glass

The woman watching the one
in the window
slips off the glove

that is life
removes the plastic film
that is smile

paints her clay hands with dye
braids her heart-strings
into rope

He appears
at her studio door
wanting a loaf or a lay

It will only take
a few minutes   he says
You'll have the whole day left

after he goes to work
the quicksand pulling her
into the luminous mundane

Grandpop Poem

Old man
why do you taunt me
with your borscht
& sour cream cheeks
& your Moses beard
& your *pianissimo* tenor
memorable
as an ode to a Jewish mother

The way you look at me
as if you misplaced
your Israel brochures
or your glasses

Salt hills glitter in your eyes
They close like candles I snuffed
Head back   you snore
to wake instantly
& shake your head
like a saucepan you wish
to empty of roaches

What is it you promise
your kiss on my lips
gentle as Azrael's wing

Azrael
your skin a damask
mottled with brown moons
the ruby rivers criss-crossing
your hands
the diamond on your pinkie

You're a poem sequence
I'll never finish
a novocaine for old rage

your holding me on your lap
your dipping the egg bread in coffee
the sputum   that ocean spray
on your chin
the phleghmy cough
the serpent tongue
the boil on your neck
the clot in your eye
the vein in your forehead
your twitching thumb
your unbuttoned fly

Sexpot

My Mother's Dress

In the women's bar
waiting for friends who

don't show up
I am my mother's daughter

in the dress she has sewn
too large like all

the dresses she said
I'd grow into

The women here form
a pin cushion of arms

this a safe room
this room a safe

each of us male
as well as female

halves of a primordial
egg once split

leaving us to search
for the goose that laid it

Turned on by these women
yet still

on the outskirts circling
the dance floor loom

postponing the shuttle
evading commitment

cautious/afraid
the knit of her skin

still expected to wear
through the rejections

in a dress that still
does not fit

The House on Stevens Street

You are thinking of selling
your tiny row
home   on Stevens Street
Young Catholics   with small children
        policemen   firemen   men who work with their
hands   are crowding out the Jews   you
    who   thirty years before   drove water
bugs   like armored tanks   from   your
                new houses

                and sank the odor
of skunk cabbage   in drug store perfume
        the fields filled now
    with houses   hand-holding paper dolls
            where   once   a boy with freckles
and red hair kissed me

                                His name
        was Teddy
                and his braces clinked

            A creaking house
                        a seething pot
brown as fresh-roast coffee
            or   Van Gogh's "Potato
    Eaters"   its Magic Pan   fragrant
        with stuffed cabbage   with cinnamon
and nutmeg
    sour with sweet   tomato married
            too young   to lemon

crullers
     hissing like souls in the
steam baths   of Gehennah
         the aunts
  pared for kitchen action
     to long-line brassieres
old women scouring nubile hens who went
  to the ovens
     ignorant as greenhorns

       our dining room table a
   dock   for Sunday refugees
each phone call an S.O.S. a ship bell
  through the fog of the mundane
   Morning post-partum
    to Saturday night gin rummy
 "Arlene dear add more water to
the soup"   you   tense
    at the ship radio

       Amos n Andy
   Al Jolson
 singing *Maa a a mee*
Jack Armstrong   The All
 American Boy Kellogg's Corn Flakes
  Breakfast
of Champions a prize-winning coupon in every
   box when
  lox   was cheap enough

to carpet bagels
wall   to wall
In The Yard (the concrete driveway shared by all)
the wash   baptized   in bluing
Father's shirts

in starch strait-jackets

braving
the midday
heat of heats

"The Girls"
sat out   on kitchen chairs   to hem
chat   tan
their flabby legs and admire
the kids
going under the hose
"Don't squirt the laundry"
The newest wife on the
block   confided

she undressed at night in
the closet   while   in the
kitchen   the day worker chewed
on fried porgies
and swallowed fish bones   for swords
then   trudged   upstairs   to grease
the bureau
and take her   snuff   covertly
while the pipes   clogged

                              and something red as
Heinz Ketchup   dripped
        down the little girls' legs to
                                        punish
                them for playing   Doctor
      while the water sacs   burst
        like birthday balloons
                        and the babies   birthed
          like prophecies

                                wee
                wood turtles
                                    with joggling heads
          the house a matchmaker
Matchmaker   Matchmaker
                        The nephew who brought home a war
          bride
                  you
                        had to kosher

                Weddings
      in the living room   the neighbors   spying
              through   the venetians   I
        your number two bride   in a sky
      blue   flat-chested dress   a flying saucer
              hat   of natural   straw
                                          the hymen
                              skimmed off my
          milk when it   came

to a premature
boil   on the mohair couch
                              I carried roses from
          Father's bush   the lawn   that grass patch
              large   as a boy friend's semen'd
handkerchief   The rabbi who said "Do you promise
              to be a good wife"
                              the same one
                         who would trim

                              the fat
          from my baby boy
                         and break bread at Father's
              funeral
       After   thirty   the cells   go
                         quickly   a bingo card   odds
              doubling
a coffee pot   boiling   over
                         Father

                         did
                              like a bad dirty joke or
          a cap   that   popped
     off the toothpaste
                         Father
our house   a ghetto   for grieving   women
                    a tombstone purchased at thirty
     payments still
                    owing   our house   so thin

after   the fat man   went to the second row
house   the first a black market
         for
           Cupid ashtrays
   for
       Bankruptcy   Death Divorce
                    matches
      to kindle a widow's
   suttee   Double Bingo

Packing
      the fireworks away in mothballs
         Goodbye   to your   sexy
    son-in-law   Mother the house needs
papering   painting
        the roof leaks rain or semen
    Tar it
   Feather   the old lumps with wallpaper
       doves   cabbage roses

        rancid as wash
         left in the Bendix
grease   tripled   in price the day-
   worker snuffed
      Hooray The War is over
Our Boys have won Our Boys (the nephews in Hercules
     condoms) cheat on their plump wives
  & pacify them with new toaster ovens
and wall

                    to wall carpet   the cruller pan
        dented   the sweet with the sour   bitter
lemons   left   overnight   in the borscht
    "Arlene   wash the walls   with bicarbonate"
                         Take two please   every four hours
                    my baby turtle

                                            halfway through
        Harvard   (you don't say)   Listen
                    Sweetheart   who needs

                                            to dig a path
            with a knife and fork   you don't
have to be an
                        Einstein
        to see
                                    the black roses mass
            on the winter white X-ray
                    A virus   they told her   something
born in   the brain   & kept under the roof until

            First Father   now
                        the number two daughter bankrupt
    of living cells   The stairs   creak
                    with her name   O   Rose of
            Forgive
                    her foot in silver sandals   two steps   up
and moving   (no dear ghost) her little
        children
                            Paper confetti   a ticker

      tape parade   The third war

                                        reigns
              the street deserted   this
your sixtieth   seventieth winter
        Ice
           that Arctic elephant   mammoth
    ice cube
Forty   the years
                you've had   possession

            of the house   or it
of you
        After thirty   rain pours
through the sieve that is roof
             greasy   as   chicken soup
            kasha barley nails teeth condoms
   trusses stresses hair white
         black dye
             old scraps

                    old rags
             potholders   dish towels
   bedspreads   the coffee-color birthmark on your leg
    & on mine   the stain in the back of/
the gap in Father's shorts   Bring bleach/Bring
   bluing vein artery valve   left ventricle   left
arm   the pain *ahhhhh*
                 Body
      the wandering minstrel   Body the pedlar

Body the paper house
                        Body the   Joker in a short deck
            Body the comic book
                      binding broken like the back of a
      whipped mule   the binders departed
                      Aunt Dora   Bubba Grandpop Uncle
Frank & Uncle Jake   Yug o sla vi a
             Czech o slo va ki a
                Ahhh h h h h

                      Sell the house
                                Sell the
curlers   brassiere   corset
                    home for old bones
        Sell the womb   Sell the car
              leave the driving to us you who
have babysat
                six rooms
      for   four decades

                      Green Eyes
            eyes green as
      the sea   in Atlantic City when I was a
                toy turtle
          Age   takes your house hurricane
sweeping   the wobbly piers   What
      can I say to   stop it   Mother
   plead
      Keep me

                    a child
The matinee's   nearly   over   Ghosts
            call   on the phone/mail ultimatums
          The roof leaks   roses rusting this Fall
We cannot keep saying
                    wrong number
            Rae
                          The neighborhood
     is   changing